MOTOR
SCOOTERS
Colour Family Album

(IWL Berlin 1960)

First published in 1998 by Veloce Publishing Plc., 33, Trinity Street, Dorchester DT1 1TT, England. Fax: 01305 268864.

ISBN: 1-901295-03-6/UPC: 36847-00103-2

British Library Cataloguing in Publication Data -
A catalogue record for this book is available from the British Library.

Typesetting (Avant Garde), design and page make-up all by Veloce on AppleMac.
Printed in Hong Kong.

MOTOR SCOOTERS
Colour Family Album

ANDREA & DAVID SPARROW

VELOCE PUBLISHING PLC
PUBLISHERS OF FINE AUTOMOTIVE BOOKS

THANKS

Thanks are due to all of the following - Marc Defrance, Yves Dumetz, Patrick Pattier, Mike and Val Dan, Martin van de Langenberg, Hans Van Beek, Rainer Langguth, Günter Wilmerdinger, Adri Smits, Jan Jansen, Sandra Da Silva, Tina Forkel, Florence Boyer, Marie-Laurenece Decke, Debbie Bollaart, Jaak Kerkhofs, Harold van Hees, Jan Vellinga, Gunter van Herreweghen, Bert Woolfink, Nathalie van der Klok, Mario Piscicelli, Pauline Chart, Alain Goulois, Bert Eeman of Galerie D'Ieteren, Shirley Pattison, Piaggio UK, Jane Palmer of Bristol Zoo, Catherine Skrzypczak, Kevin Mapp, Samantha Smith, Associated British Ports; Southampton, Oliver Körber, Ella and Freddy.

(Zundapp Bella 200 1962)

CONTENTS

INTRODUCTION

While we were working on the Vespa and Lambretta Colour Family Albums, we met lots of people for whom scootering was a way of life. One thing that surprised us was the extent to which even the most passionate of marque fanatics was interested in scooters of other types, and scootering in general.

This book does not set out to be an encyclopedia of scooters, or to give definitive coverage of every model a manufacturer ever made. Vespa & Lambretta may be the ones that everyone has heard of, but there are other, no less interesting, stories to be told of other manufacturers, and of other countries. Manufacturers which spring to mind today might be Piaggio and Peugeot – although not everyone would know that Piaggio was Vespa, and that Peugeot made scooters in the 1950s. Many manufacturers are simply no longer in existence, or have reinvented themselves as something completely different. So if you remember a Rumi, courted with a Cushman or longed for a Lohner, worry not. We intend that this slim book be Scooters, volume one.

(Piatti - Belgium - 1955)

6

ORIGIN OF THE SPECIES

1

Although the austerity of postwar years brought the scooter's finest hour, the origins of the species go back much further to the early days of motoring history. Among the first real scooters were the Motoped of 1915 and the Autoped of 1917, both from the USA. They were unsophisticated affairs, with a small motor driving the front wheel,

Although not a contender for the fast lane, the Skootamota - and its contemporaries - excited a great deal of interest: the motor scooter had arrived. (Skootamota 1919)

but they were fun to ride and were, perhaps, a status symbol of a kind. There were doubtless those of an older generation who believed that the sanity of the world was at stake on account of them, and that they represented the beginning of the end. On the other side of the Atlantic the firm of Krupp was making a similar machine in Germany and Norlow was doing the same in England, where partner Sir Henry Norman used his scooter to get to the House of Lords.

One of the best known of the early scooters also came from England: the ABC Skootamota, the brainchild of an eccentric engineer rejoicing in the wonderfully English name of Granville Bradshaw. Mr Bradshaw (surely we must call him that?) fitted his scooter with a 125cc single-cylinder four-stroke engine. Produced from 1919 until 1923, the Skootamota was capable of a stately 40kph (24mph). It became quite well-known, and was popular not only in England - sales in France were in the region of a thousand examples. The scooter also became the preferred mode of transport for celebrities with an eye for a photo-opportunity.

The Skootamota was also sold as a working vehicle: with the addition of a luggage compartment in front of the rear wheel, it was deemed an ideal delivery vehicle. There were many other variations on a scooter theme to choose from, too. The Reynolds Runabout was fitted with a 270cc engine and could reach speeds of 65kph

(40mph) - a frightening prospect. The Lumen company of Paris offered a similar scooter to the Skootamota, but with larger wheels and, although it had a larger 150cc engine, speed capability was much less: a maximum of 25kph (15mph).

Monet & Goyon produced scooters which they claimed were ideally suited to French roads - the Vélauto and Super-Vélauto. The Briggs and Stratton from the USA and the Autoscoot from England were similar in style, too. From England also came the Autoglider (built by the Townsend company), the Kenilworth (from Booth Bros of Coventry) and the strikingly modern-looking Unibus (from the Gloucestershire Aircraft company in Cheltenham). DKW produced two scooters in Germany, the Golem and the Lomos.

Most of these early scooters were built in decent numbers only until the mid-1920s, after which there was very little to report on the scooter scene until after World War 2.

The renaissance of the scooter, and the reasons why it occured are well understood. The Vespa was created because Enrico Piaggio needed to find a quickly saleable product to get his bombed-out factory back on its feet – something that could be manufactured without the need to retrain his staff. The success of the Vespa owes much to Piaggio's vision in commissioning Corradino D'Ascanio to design and engineer a scooter. In a similar fashion, the Lambretta was born of the need to get the

The Skootamota's 125cc single-cylinder four-stroke engine propelled it to some 40kph (24mph). This example is kept running thanks to several much younger scooters, including a Vespa which (inset) donated a spare carburettor. (Skootamota 1919)

Italian economy going again as quickly as possible.

The 1950s and 1960s became the golden age for the scooter because a whole new way of life was unfolding during this time, and the scooter was very much part of it all. Great social changes were taking place in the scooter's homeland of Italy. Previous younger generations would have tended to marry, settle down and raise their children in or around their home town. Cheap transport, such as the scooter provided, brought a new social life, involving journeys to towns and cities, a broadening of outlook and the end of the old order. No wonder many felt threatened by the scooter and the extent of its influence.

Scooters may have started life as a practical and utilitarian answer to a transport problem, but they soon achieved symbolic status for the young (although still a good remedy for those transport problems, of course). In fact, to be a scooterist it was only necessary to be young at heart. There are many images from the 1950s of the archetypal grandma, dressed in black, shopping basket full of

Vehicles such as the Monotrace paved the way for later, workable, solutions to transport problems but, in a dog-eat-dog world, they became museum pieces. The small outrigger wheels lifted off the ground once balance was attained; a concept that didn't catch on then, but which has been revisited recently on futuristic car-motorcycles. (Monotrace 1926-28)

vegetables, skimming over the cobblestones on her Vespa. What was the story? Had she always been a modern, or did she reluctantly borrow that Vespa from her grandson one day and never look back? The scooter was a liberating influence for anyone and everyone prepared to try it. For women it performed a particularly valuable function.

The traditional roles were no longer cast in stone; women were taking on careers, supporting themselves, choosing when to get married and have children (or not to), and

the scooter could provide independence. The scooter's advantages over the motor-car or motorcycle – economy, ease of riding, parking and maintenance - ensured its success at that moment in history.

The cult of the scooter soon spread from Italy to the rest of Europe. Licence agreements for the manufacture of the major marques were soon changing hands until, by the late 1950s, scooters were being produced all over the world. Eastern-bloc cloning gave rise to machines such as the Vjatka - a USSR-style Vespa. In India the scooter offered a practical solution to the huge and ever-growing problem of transport, and there the commercial variations, like the three-wheeled Vespa APE, were soon taken up as delivery vans and taxis. In the USA the scooter was well established, with makes such as Cushman and Salisbury in great demand. Japan was also discovering the scooter's potential - their first home-grown product was the Fuji Rabbit, launched in 1947, closely followed by the Mitsubishi Pigeon.

During the relatively prosperous 1960s, the scooter took on a different role. Any self-respecting British teenager must be either a Mod (uniform parka, neat haircut, a collection of The Who records and a scooter - preferably

Cafe society. Scooters were stylish, but not snobbish. (Vespa)

Lambretta) or a Rocker (uniform leathers, no haircut, a collection of Elvis records and a motorbike). To the former, the opposition was uncouth. To the latter, the scooter-boys were wimps. Bank Holidays in Brighton were no place for the faint-hearted, children, or small dogs. Did anarchy reign, as so many politicians and armchair experts believed? Not at all!

By the end of the 1960s the scooter's heyday was drawing to a close. Lambretta ceased production in 1971, and most European manufacturers had moved on to other things. Vespa continued in production, however, and moved forward with the introduction of their New Line in 1977.

It was not until the 1990s that the scooter began to reinvent itself. New materials, computer-aided design and new safety requirements shaped the image of the new machines. Demand was being created by economic factors, by the problems of traffic volume (especially in cities) and by a very real concern over 'green' issues which is not just been a passing phase. Today's scooters are sleek and ergonomic, too heavily car-styled for some tastes, but

Beloved of 1960s British Mods, and star of the film Quadrophenia, *the Lambretta still has a huge following today - and not just with those Mod grandfathers! (Lambretta SX200 1966)*

Cheap to buy, economical to run and small enough to deliver in the tiniest of streets. Commercials based on the scooter - most famously those of Vespa and Lambretta - spelled success for many small businesses. (Piaggio APE Commercial)

practical, economic and fun. Piaggio's Zip & Zip, for example, provides the best of both worlds for commuting into town. A conventional engine propels you to the outskirts, where you switch to battery power for quiet, pollution-free town travel. Peugeot's Scootelec drives you around town all day on battery power; then you simply plug it into the mains at night for a complete recharge.

At the other end of the scale are machines such as Piaggio's 150cc Hexagon and Yamaha's hugely powerful 250cc Majesty, which bridge the gap between traditional motorcycling and more conventional scootering. The choice of which scooter to buy really is a case of 'horses for courses' (or, perhaps, whatever scoots the purpose?)

That certain Italian style – of which the scooter has always been a very important part. (Vespa)

A green machine - the Piaggio Zip & Zip has a conventional engine with a hidden surprise: the ability to run on battery power, too. (Piaggio Zip & Zip)

Towards the end of the 1960s, there was a move towards smaller, lightweight scooters with small engines: easy to ride and inexpensive to run. (Lambretta Vega 75cc 1969)

The Vespa was, and still is, the scooter that even the philistines have heard of, and the GS was the classic Vespa. (Vespa GS, 1962 on)

PEUGEOT

2

Although Peugeot celebrated a century of motor manufacture in 1990, the history of the company stretches back to 1810, when the Peugeot brothers from the Doubs region of France converted an old flour mill into a workshop and manufactured steel springs for the local clock and watchmaking industry. Their business grew steadily, and diversified somewhat over the next half-century. As well as springs, they made tools, coffee grinders, sewing machines and even corset stays! By the mid 1880s, however, the Peugeot company was hard at work manufacturing the latest transport fashion – the bicycle - and was gathering a reputation for it far and wide.

The Peugeot steam-driven tricycle was one of the sensations of the Paris exhibition of 1889, but Peugeot realised that the future lay with the new internal combustion

The Speedfight takes centre stage as a best-seller.
(Speedfight 1997)

engine, and the following year introduced their first motor car – a quadricycle fitted with a Daimler engine.

Naturally, one of the first concerns of the new motoring fraternity at the turn of the century was to see who was fastest, who could go the farthest, and who was the most frugal. Peugeots took part in an early run from Paris to Brest, covering 2100km in 139 hours. In 1896, Armand Peugeot formed *La Société des Automobiles Peugeot*. There was another, rather dubious, distinction for the company that year: the first ever car to be stolen was a Peugeot!

The Peugeot concern continued to grow throughout the first half of the century. Although then a firmly established car manufacturer, the company did not desert the two-wheel market; demand for Peugeot bicycles was as great as ever.

World War 2 brought inevitable changes. The days of lavish lifestyles and expensive motoring were gone. In order to survive, manufacturers had to look to affordable means of transport for the ordinary working-person – and the ordinary working-person was really very hard-pressed financially.

In 1948 Peugeot launched its small car - the hugely popular 203, which would be manufactured until 1960. its designers were looking at other forms of motoring also, and began research into the possibilities of a scooter. It was not the Peugeot style to rush things. Peugeot's reputation was built on solid foundations,

With its narrower apron, the C model may have offered less protection against wind, but the headlamp on the handlebars certainly gave better illumination.
(S.57 1959)

21

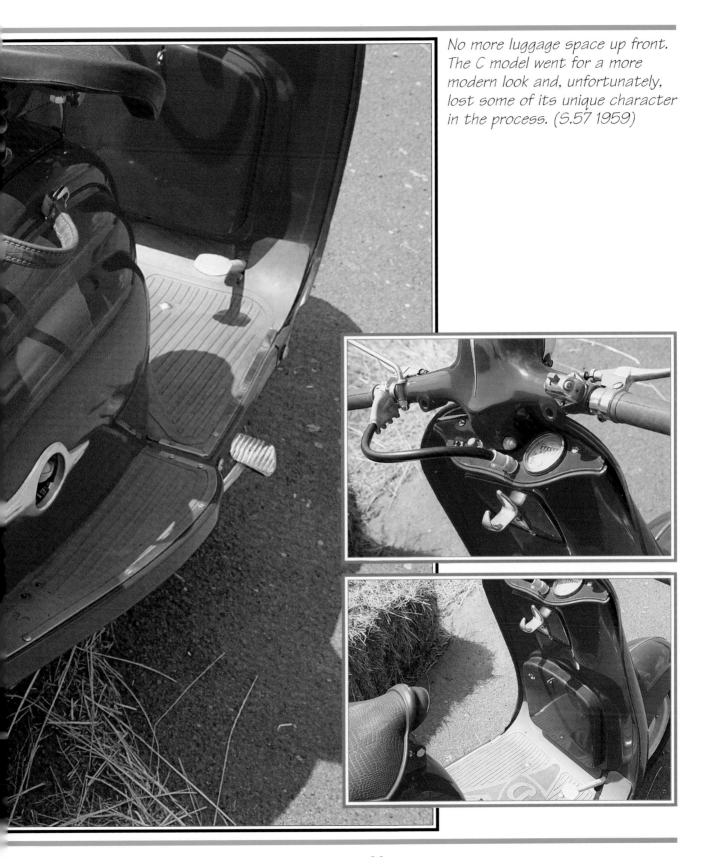

No more luggage space up front. The C model went for a more modern look and, unfortunately, lost some of its unique character in the process. (S.57 1959)

Leg protection on the Peugeot was good, thanks to the wide, curved apron. (S.157 1953)

Peugeot's small car – the 203 – had been in production for five years when the company introduced the S.157 scooter. Its engine was based on their P.55 moped unit.
(S.157 1953)

and it was not a company to hasten an ill-prepared Italian clone into production merely to jump on the bandwagon.

The prototype Peugeot scooter was unveiled to the press in 1953, and introduced officially at the Paris Salon in October that year. The S.55's 125cc, 4.6hp engine was based on the unit which powered the P.55 moped. The frame was a classic tubular design, clothed in unusual but very practical bodywork. From the front, at least, the Peugeot looked very different to most other scooters, with its large front platform - a luggage compartment with a lid - on which a decent amount of luggage could be carried), and its car-like legshield shape and headlamp pod. Only a few S.55s were made in the first year, and, at the Paris Salon in 1954, an updated version was introduced.

The S.57 differed from its predecessor in that it had a hand gearchange, rather than pedal. 1955 brought a 150cc version, the S.157, its engine based this time on Peugeot's P.155. This model was intended primarily for export markets. The same year saw the introduction of the

The Peugeot logo, a distinctive, backward-facing letter 'P,' adorns the handlebars. Early Peugeots had a pedal gearchange, whereas later models had a hand-operated change. (S.55 1954)

Opposite - The first Peugeots had a very different profile to other scooters. The flat area over the front wheel, with handles for securing luggage, was particularly useful. (S.55 1954)

S.57 AL (for *allégé* - light), with less luggage space up front, no pillion seat (this is where the luggage went), no speed-ometer and narrower tyres.

The Paris Salon was always the focus for new models and updates for established ones, and the home-grown prod-ucts from companies such as Peugeot were among those most eagerly awaited. In October 1956 the spotlight was on a modernised version of Peugeot's popular scooter, now called S.57 B. The fixed headlamp had been moved up to the handlebars, where its directional abilities helped greatly to illuminate those notorious bends in French country lanes. The other notable change was the addition of a large air filter, with its attached pipework protruding from the left hand side of the bodywork. The following year saw the intro-duction of the S.57 C, which was to be sold alongside the B model. Gone was the fixed front mudguard with its distinc-tive platform, to be replaced by a moving front mudguard, without room to transport even a cheese or two. The engine power was increased slightly to 5.1hp, and wheel size increased, too.

Although they may not have captured the imagina-tion or the export markets in the same way as some of the Italian scooter marques, the

Much easier to park than a car and not such hard work as a bicycle. (50cc 1997)

Peugeot were without a scooter on their books for more than twenty years, but have returned to the market with a whole range of good-looking, practical scooters for the 1990s. (Zenith 1997)

Peugeots of the 1950s were extremely popular in their home country and are still highly-regarded today. As well as their conventional badging, they were sold under the name of Griffon/ FMC, with the addition of 500 to the model number, giving S.555, S.557 and S.657.

After a gap of some thirty years, Peugeot began building scooters again in the 1980s, this time, of course, with all the advantages that new materials and production methods could provide.

The Metropolis 50cc models, the jazzy-looking Rapido and Fox 50 introduced in 1992, made an immediate impression, especially with the younger generation of scooterists. Such scooters are capable of just 30mph in restricted form, but top speed can be increased 50 per cent for those riders who legally qualify to have their machines derestricted. Today's range includes smart, lightweight, practical bikes, such as the 50cc two-stroke automatic Zenith which is easy and comfortable to ride. It is fitted with ten-inch wheels, has telescopic front forks and front disc brake and is available in a choice of bright, classy colours.

The Buxy - a strange name for English speakers - is an off-road style 50cc automatic that comes in bright purple with chunky tyres and with a whole range of somewhat macho accessories. It also comes in an RS version with normal tyres and a red colour scheme. The equally oddly-named Squab is another off-road style, air-cooled automatic, with an advantage over previous models in that it has helmet storage under the seat - the previous lack of which had annoyed and mystified Peugeot owners in equal measure. Anti-theft security is provided by an integral snake-lock which can be pulled out from the frame and wrapped around a suitable fixed object, or around the rear wheel.

The Peugeot Speedfight earned itself the distinction of being Britain's best-selling scooter during 1997. The LC is a 50cc two-stroke, but water-cooled, and has approached the problem of theft with the integral lock, as fitted to the Squab. The LCT model also has a key immobiliser system. The latest addition to the Speedfight range is the 100 (again, a two-stroke auto, but air-cooled) which is capable of around 100kph (60mph) and has all the security features of the LCT, but is still priced reasonably and is inexpensive to run.

And then there is the Scootelec. Designed for city use, this amazing, good-looking little scooter, with a top speed of 45kph (just under 30mph), is electric. Use it during the day, then plug it into the mains at night. A complete charge takes just five hours, and it will be ready for another 45km the following morning!

The Squab has an inbuilt anti-theft snake-lock - you only need a piece of railing that's not already taken. (Squab 1997)

The Peugeot's lines are individual, in a very French manner. (S.55 1954)

Peugeots benefit from great attention to detail: the numberplate on this scooter is not just tacked on afterwards - its an integral part of the design (S.55 1953)

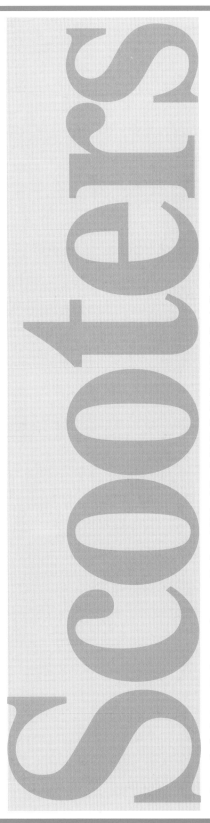

3

PIATTI

The British *en masse* must be forgiven for not falling head-over-heels in love with the scooter. This is not due to traditional reserve or conservatism; nor does it stem from the fear that taking on board things Italian inevitably leads to kissing people in the street you hardly know. It has much to do with the weather - scooters suffer the same market resistance as convertibles in northern Europe . So it is to the credit of companies such as Douglas, BSA and Triumph that they were prepared to give the scooter a try in Britain.

The Piatti first appeared at the Brussels Salon in 1952. Designed by London-based Italian engineer, Vincenzo Piatti, it was taken up enthusiastically by the Brussels-based *Les Anciens Etablissements D'Ieteren*. This company had a long and distinguished history, having been founded in 1805 as the maker of fine horse-drawn coaches. With the advent of the motorcar, the company expanded into this new market and, by the mid-1920s, was building elegant coachwork on chassis by manufacturers such as

Duesenburg, Hispano-Suiza and Rolls-Royce. Anticipating the move towards mass-produced cars, the company also acquired distribution rights from American manufacturers. After World War 2 it became the Belgian importer for VW, Porsche and Studebaker, and, later, Audi for which it is still the major importer and distributor in Belgium.

The intention of *D'Ieteren* was to build some 5000 Piattis in the space of a few years. Production got under way during 1954, but the expected sales failed to materialise. By then, the postwar scooter boom had already peaked in Belgium; the Vespa, among others, was well entrenched, but the market for small cars was on the increase, and four wheels would shortly be stealing the limelight from two.

Production of the Piatti in Britain began in 1956. The Cyclemaster company of Byfleet in Surrey manufactured small two-stroke engines for fitting to bicycles. The company was unusually forward-thinking in its approach to the scooter market. The majority of the British two-wheeler

The Piatti is remembered kindly by those who rode one in the 1950s, though they'll remember a few problems, too. (UK 1957)

industry was very sceptical about scooters, with few manufacturers prepared to take the plunge, but Cyclemaster created an efficient service network, not just in Britain, but in twenty-six other countries. The company spent money on publicity, too, so that the Piatti would have the best possible start. The sales material mixed its metaphors, claiming that the Piatti was 'as sturdy as a young lion, light as a feather,' and proudly proclaiming it 'The Scooter of Tomorrow.'

Initial sales were encouraging, but, in truth, the Piatti was underdeveloped and could be decidedly unreliable. Overheating was a major problem; engine protection was insufficient to prevent dirt from getting into the carburettor and the gearchange mechanism had a tendency to sheer off, as did the kickstart quadrants. The use of screws rather than bolts caused enormous frustration for both owners and mechanics: slots soon became damaged, and many screws could not be removed or tightened with the engine *in situ*. Poor quality of materials and inadequate quality control in the factory did little to help matters.

The Piatti was not without its good points, and received some good reviews in the press. The engine was advanced for its time - a low-slung, pivoted horizontal 125cc unit with an in-line three-speed gearbox and a chain-drive in an oil bath. The unit's 4.75hp gave a top speed of 78kph, with fuel consumption a respectable 50km/l. (Piatti had also designed a two-speed 98cc version, which did not go into serious production.) Protection for the rider was excellent: the detachable windshield had a canvas section fixed below, which left no draughty gaps between handlebars and legshield.

The Piatti was comfortable to ride, not least because adjustments could easily be made to suit rider and load.

Although it looks strange, the addition of a pannier at the front was a very practical move, and the weight distribution was well thought-out. (B 1955)

Detail styling and the Piatti's instruments and controls have a strong 1950's flavour as do the red and cream paint finish. (UK 1957)

British Piattis came in a better, brighter range of colours than their Belgian counterparts, helping them make an altogether more positive first impression. (UK 1957)

A good idea in theory: to work on the engine of your Piatti, simply lay it on its side. In practice, the process was a lot more complicated and messy! (Belgian 1955 above, UK 1957 opposite)

Access to the carburettor, with the Piatti in an upright position. (UK 1957)

The height of the handlebars and seat were adjustable, and the rear shock absorber mounting had three positions on the chassis, to alter compensate for different loads. The twist-grip gearchange had click-stops, so gear selections were easily accomplished. Weight distribution was excellent, with the option of fitting a capacious pannier at the front, while additional storage space could be found in the seat and spare wheel. The steering could easily be locked with a simple padlock.

The Piatti was designed so that engine maintenance could be carried out by tipping the scooter on its side, after first closing a seal on the fuel cap. Unfortunately, this idea - brilliant in theory - was not received enthusiastically by Piatti owners. It actually made maintenance even more of a chore, as luggage had to be moved from the carrier, and it was virtually necessary to lie in the road to get at anything.

Although the Piatti's disad-

Cream details on the red paintwork of Mike Dan's beautifully restored Piatti add a finishing touch to the quirky scooter. (UK 1957)

vantages may seem to have outweighed its advantages, it was a good-looking scooter, especially in its British livery - it came in a choice of colours and two-tone colour schemes. (The Belgian version only ever appeared in light grey.) Its striking body shape makes the Piatti one of the most unusual scooters. The nose of its cigar-shaped monocoque body has something of the dolphin about it; the legshield and seat interrupt the line fore and aft and the tiny seven-inch wheels are almost hidden within the body. Unlike many of its contemporaries, the

Piatti does not look as if it has simply borrowed elements of its shape and line from other marques - it is unique.

For some time it was believed that 5000 or so Piattis were built in Belgium, but this figure is actually only the intended production. In fact, figures from the Brussels factory indicate that just 805 were built before production ended in 1957, although sales in Britain reached 15,000.

The Belgian scooters never found an export market of any kind, and their British counterparts had only slightly more success. In 1957 they made a

brief foray into the French market, when Ets Ch Escoffier exhibited several imported examples at the Paris Salon. Unfortunately, difficulties with administration soon put an end to the idea.

Cyclemaster attempted to solve the worst of the Piatti's problems with development of a Mark 2 version, but this was destined never to go into production. Sadly, passable home sales and a good press were not sufficient to secure the Piatti's future. The Cyclemaster factory closed in 1958, and production of the Piatti came to an end.

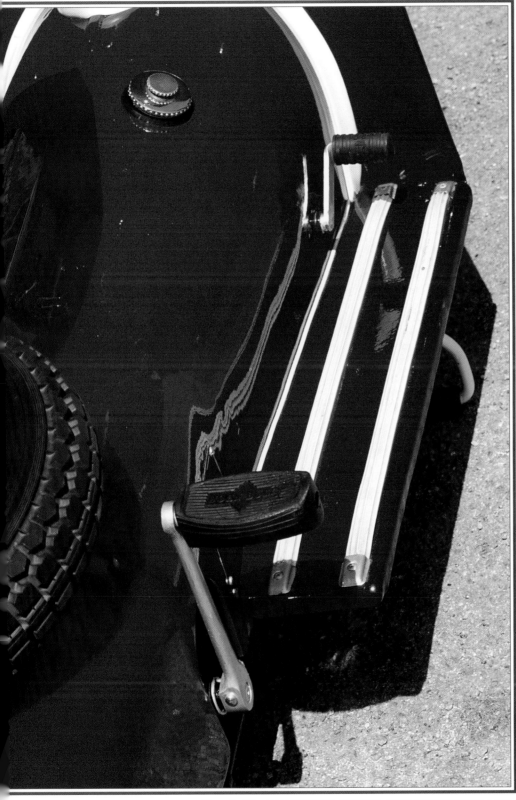

Cream details on the red paintwork of Mike Dan's beautifully restored Piatti add a finishing touch to the quirky scooter. (UK 1957)

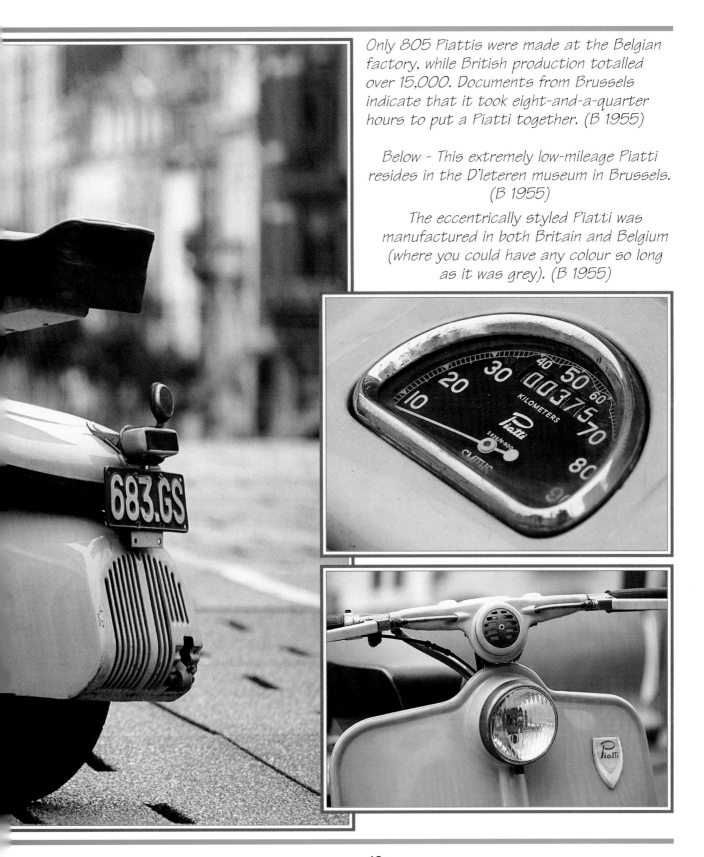

Only 805 Piattis were made at the Belgian factory, while British production totalled over 15,000. Documents from Brussels indicate that it took eight-and-a-quarter hours to put a Piatti together. (B 1955)

Below - This extremely low-mileage Piatti resides in the D'Ieteren museum in Brussels. (B 1955)

The eccentrically styled Piatti was manufactured in both Britain and Belgium (where you could have any colour so long as it was grey). (B 1955)

The Piatti's seat and handlebars were both height-adjustable, a useful feature many more-famous scooter makes didn't offer.
(UK 1957)

BITRI

4

Although the Netherlands is not noted for its scooter industry, many different makes and models were imported. In addition to the major Italian contenders, Heinkel, Zündapp and Gogo-Isaria found a ready market there. Just as there were manufacturers in the Netherlands prepared to give the microcar a try, so there were those willing to back the scooter.

The Sparta was a scooter/moped hybrid from Apeldoorn, and was produced from 1953. It came in two engine sizes: 50cc and 98cc. In similar vein were the Motormeyer, fitted with a 70cc engine, and the 118cc Stockvis. But the truly scooter-shaped scooter from the Netherlands was the Bitri. Manufactured by the *Nederlandse Scooterfabrik NV* of Dokkum in the north of the country, it was introduced at the end of 1954.

The Bitri was built around a simple tubular frame, and sported bodywork of aluminium, very much in the classic Lambretta shape. It was a comfortable scooter to ride, with helical springs front and rear and a good firm seat. The first Bitris were powered by a 4.5hp 118cc Ilo engine and had a two-speed gearbox, with hand-operated gearchange. The setup was soon changed to a more powerful, 6.7hp 150cc unit, with three-speed gearbox and pedal gearchange. From 1957, a further version was available, this time fitted with a 10.2hp 200cc Sachs engine and a four-speed gearbox. An electric starter was offered as an option. De Luxe versions were also available, giving a smart two-tone paint option. The Bitri was reliable and highly-regarded by its owners, but never sold in vast numbers. Production soldiered on into the 1960s.

The Bitri has something of the Lambretta about its shape. It was a good workhorse, especially with the 200cc engine fitted. It was reliable and was easy to work on when the need did arise. (200cc 1958)

There are few Bitris still in existence; like a rare bird, they are seldom seen and hardly ever photographed. This example still lives in the Netherlands. (200cc 1958)

The town crest of Dokkum in Freisland, home town of the Bitri. (200cc 1958)

54

This page and opposite - details of the Bitri's engine, foot pedals and instruments. 118cc and 150cc Ilo engines powered the first Bitris; the Sachs 200cc arrived as an option in 1957, along with a four-speed gearbox. (200cc 1958)

Introduced in 1954, the Bitri was produced into the 1960s before it reached the end of the road. (200cc 1958)

GILERA

Motorcycle manufacturers have often been reluctant to take the step into scooter production, although the move might seem to be an easy one. With sales and servicing networks already in place, and a good deal of common ground between the workings of the motorcycle and the scooter, they might have been expected to launch into the scooter market with enthusiasm. However, whether it was an emotional response or a hard-nosed business decision, the motorcycling fraternity generally - with notable exceptions, of course - has had its suspicions about the scooter and its place in the market.

The Gilera company was founded in 1909 by Giuseppe Gilera, who started out producing bicycle-derived, single-cylinder, four-stroke machines, which he raced with considerable success. He built up his business in Arore, in Milan, and this grew throughout the early years into a well-known and respected motorcycle manufacturing concern.

During the 1930s there were numerous racing victories for Gilera machines, including the Grand Prix of Nations, Italian Championships and European Championships. After the war, there were more successes; the arrival of a new four-cylinder machine heralding a string of victories in the 500cc category, including six World Championships, six Italian Championships and numerous road-race victories. The single-cylinder machines also notched up numerous victories, both on the track and in road races.

Specially adapted Gileras were supreme in the record-breaking battles that were fought so hard in that era. In 1937 Gilera had captured the speed record of 274kph and, two years later, set a one-hour record of 205kph which stood until 1957 when they bettered it by no less than 22kph. In the same year, they went on to set two more one-hour records. In Enduro racing Gilera also enjoyed some resounding successes over the years, taking many medals in the Motorcycle Olympics from the late 1940s right through to the mid-1970s, when Gilera withdrew from endurance racing, concentrating instead

The Runner - latest in a long line of Gilera products. (Runner 1997)

You couldn't get a car through here ...
(Runner 1997)

The Runner's instruments are organised car-fashion. They are very easy to read, with a full-range of gauges and warning lights ...

Space for a helmet, and a little more besides. One criticism of some modern scooters is that there's nowhere safe to leave the headgear. (Runner 1997)

Maybe 'Dark Dream' is another name that loses something in the translation nightmare. (Runner 1997)

on motocross. Here, too, some successful machines were developed, including a remarkable 36hp 125cc two-cylinder introduced in 1980 - which promptly had to be abandoned when the rules changed to exclude multi-cylinder engines! Nonetheless, Gilera wins continued until 1985, when the firm withdrew from motocross competitions. The remainder of the decade saw Gilera wins in a number of off-road rallies, including the gruelling Paris-Dakar event.

Gilera's first foray into scooter manufacturing occurred in 1962, with the introduction of the G50. This single-seater was a direct competitor of, and bore a close resemblance to, the Vespa 50. The main difference between the two was that the G50 was powered by a four-stroke unit, which was fitted on the opposite side to that of the Vespa. The following year, a more powerful 80cc version was introduced, this time with a two-person seat. Both Gileras remained in production until 1968. The following year Gilera was bought by Piaggio, which relaunched production at the Acore factory around a new range of mopeds and light two-strokes aimed at the sporting market. Piaggio also reopened Gilera's racing division, which immediately attracted worldwide attention with victories over Japanese competition.

The 50cc Gilera Runner was introduced in the summer of 1997, and two more powerful versions - fitted with 125cc and 180cc engines - followed later in the year. Gilera's

The simple clean lines of an engine/transmission unit of the 1990s - somewhat different to the exposed plumbing and cabling of fifty years ago. (Runner 1997)

The Runner is too high to be a step-through, unless you are incredibly tall.
(Runner 1997)

motorcycling heritage is recalled in the styling and construction of the Runner. A special frame is used to produce a riding position which gives the sensation of motorcycle riding, but without the need for gearchanging and clutch work. The larger engines give a feeling of motorcycle performance, too, but with the economy and lower running costs for which scooters have long been renowned.

The fuel tank (which can be filled without disturbing the seat) and the battery are fitted into the central tunnel between the rider's legs, which makes getting onto the Runner more of a hop-through than a step-through for all but the longest of legs. There is a surprisingly large amount of luggage space available under the seat, which is comfortable for rider and pillion passenger. Warm air (provided courtesy of the water-cooled engine) can be vented to unfreeze the rider's shins - a luxury which hardened bikers label 'sissy,' but most sensible folk think is a jolly good idea.

The Runner's twelve-inch wheels are fitted with racing-style tyres, which add greatly to its roadholding abilities. It is fitted with a disc brake at the front and a drum at the rear,

The SKP is light, bright, practical and fun. The ultimate weapon? - it probably depends on the enemy. (SKP 1997)

while the front suspension features upside-down telescopic forks linked to a single shock absorber at the rear. In all, the Runner is fun to ride, and has received favourable press comment. *Scootering* magazine summed it up as 'a good-looking machine which is extremely user-friendly.'

The SKP, introduced at the same time as the Runner, is an

The SKP has strong and aggressive rear end styling. (SKP 1997)

air-cooled 50cc machine, with an off-road style geared towards the younger end of the scooter market. The SKP was originally called the 'Stalker' - the name by which it is known elsewhere in Europe - but the inappropriateness of that name led to a rechristening for the British market. Gilera also produce a retro-styled 50cc - the Eaglet - with handlebars of the old style, large seat and chrome finishing.

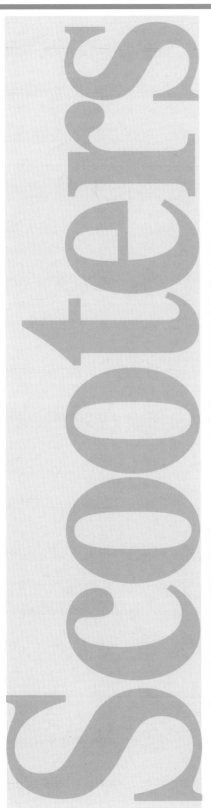

IWL

In 1953 *VEB Industriewerke Ludwigsfelde* (known as IWL) embarked on the development of a scooter. The DDR (as it was then) was anxious to keep up with the west, and inexpensive mobility was a pressing concern in every country, west or east.

The results of IWL's labours went into production in February 1955. This was the Pitty, a very strange-looking scooter indeed, which was produced for barely a year before being replaced by the Wiesel. The Wiesel was of a more conventional shape, and stayed in production for three years.

The next scooter from IWL was the SR19 Berlin, fitted with a new 7.5hp 143cc MZ engine. The Berlin was a sturdy scooter, capable of a top speed of 82kph (50mph). Production began in May 1959. IWL intended that 30,000 scooters should be built during

The Berlin was the third of four scooters made by IWL, after the Pitty and the Wiesel. (Berlin 1960)

Left & above - East Germany was anxious to keep up with the west in terms of the quality and desirability of its scooters. (Berlin 1960)

The Berlin was a good-looking, rugged scooter. This two-tone paint scheme shows the design to good advantage. (Berlin 1960)

Echos of the Lambretta, and of the Zundapp Bella too? (Berlin 1960)

the first year, so it was necessary to start off at a good, steady rate, gradually increasing daily production as much as possible.

Another target that IWL had set for itself was to earn a good international reputation, and thus create a thriving export market. To achieve this, it ensured that Berlins were to be seen at international scooter meetings whenever possible, and that word reached the ears of the maximum number of scooter enthusiasts.

In 1960 there was a 'trip to the tropics,' involving the Berlin and the IWL 'Campi' trailer. As well as raising awareness of IWL and its products, the trip was a useful test of performance under quite arduous conditions. The itinerary took in Egypt early in June, then Iran until the middle of August. The test involved a drive of over 2000km for two Berlins.

In parallel with the test runs, IWL also set about improving the quality of its product. The first export orders arrived later that year, with sales to Cuba, Egypt, Holland, Spain, Finland, Uruguay, Turkey, the USSR and Guinea. Popularity of the Berlin grew quite considerably over the next few years; production continued until the end of November 1962, with almost 114,000 machines manufactured in all.

The Berlin's controls were easy to reach and simple to operate; it was considered comfortable and sturdy as well. (Berlin 1960)

IWL wanted as many people as possible to see and appreciate its scooters, so the company appeared at scooter-meets whenever possible. (Berlin 1960)

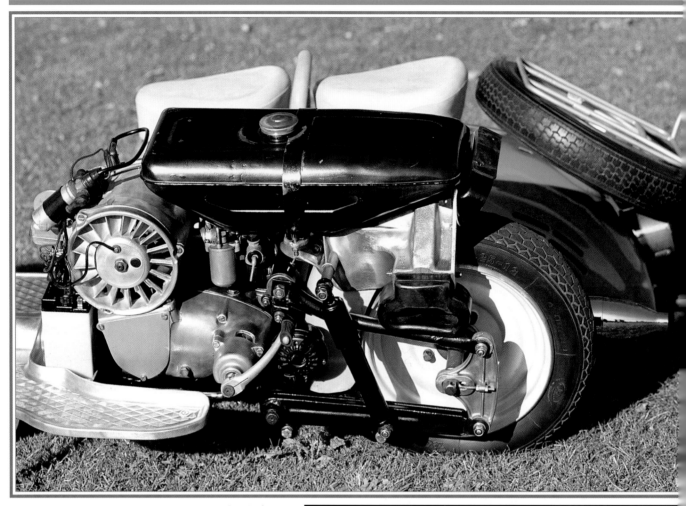

Maintenance access to the Berlin's engine was excellent: the rear section of the body lifted off completely. (Berlin 1960)

The Troll, like the Berlin before it, was fitted with a 143cc (nominally 150cc) engine, made by Motorradwerk Zschopau. (Troll 1963)

Nothing to do with Nordic gnomes, the Troll was simply a shortened form of Tourennroller. (Troll 1963)

IWL made a great effort with the quality of its products, especially with build quality and attention to detail. (Troll 1963)

The Berlin's replacement was to be the Troll 1 (short for *Tourenroller*), which began production at the beginning of January 1963. It was fitted with a new engine made by *Motorradwerk Zschopau*, a 9.5hp 143cc unit which gave the Troll a top speed of 90kph (54mph). The Troll 1 - so called from the beginning, so that modifications could be brought out as Troll 2, 3, etc. - was a tough, reliable scooter. It was comfortable and durable, but stayed in production for just two years, during which over 56,500 machines were built. Sadly, there never was a Troll 2 and the last Troll 1 rolled off the production line on 24 December 1964. IWL had been building scooters for ten years, during which time a total of almost 240,000 machines had been produced.

Right & pages 84/85 - Troll and Campi trailer make a very practical combination. (Troll 1963, with Campi trailer)

Details of the Troll 1: who knows what features Troll 2 might have brought? (Troll 1963)

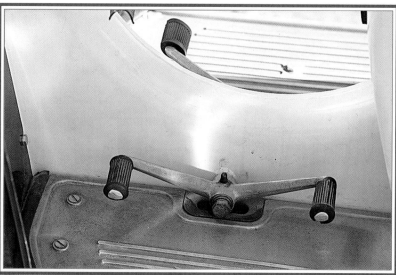

ZÜNDAPP

7

In contrast to the reticence of most motorcycle manufacturers, some took the plunge and entered the scooter market - and the decision paid off handsomely. Zündapp first looked at scooters at the start of the 1950s and was convinced that the two-wheeled craze then taking Italy by storm could take off in the German market, too.

The *Zünder-und Apparatebau GMBH* was founded in 1917 by Dr Fritz Neumeyer and F Krupp, to make electrical equipment. But Krupp remained with the company for only two years, and Neumeyer was soon looking for a change of direction. In 1921 the company - its long name now shortened to Zündapp - began the manufacture of motorcycles, which rapidly earned a good reputation and, by 1938, 200,000 had rolled off the production lines.

During the World War 2 years, Zündapp turned its attention to manufacturing motorcycles for the military, and, at the end of hostilities, had the task of rebuilding its bombed-out factory. By 1948 the firm was under way again,

manufacturing sewing machines. A new factory for this purpose, and for the manufacture of mopeds, was opened in 1951.

It was at this time that Zündapp decided to look closely at the new transport sensation taking Italy by storm - the motor scooter. Prototypes (some with more potential for success than others) were commissioned. Zündapp believed that the German market was ready for a home-grown scooter, and that it was the company to deliver the goods.

The scooter made its debut at the Frankfurt show in 1953. As Zündapp was a long-established concern with an excellent reputation, the two-wheeled world was on tenterhooks, waiting to see what had been created. The answer was the Bella, an attractive, chunky scooter which bore more than a passing resemblance to the Moto Parilla scooter of the time. Its motorcycle heritage showed too, for the Bella had large, twelve-inch wheels and a pedal gearchange, and its styling, with large wheelarch and tunnel-like mid-section,

The Zundapps were solid and well-built, but nonetheless attractive, with some interesting colour schemes. (Bella R153 1956)

suggested motorcycles also. The 150cc air-cooled two-stroke engine produced 7hp, and was capable of 80kph (50mph). Later that year a 200cc, 10hp Bella was introduced. In addition to its more powerful engine, this version had better electrics, and the headlamp - positioned midway between handlebars and mudguard on the 150 - was moved higher up the front apron, with the horn beneath. The two Bellas certainly made a good impression: they looked solid and reliable, and the reassurance of a good,

well-known motorcycling name helped the marketing no end. An electric-start version of the 200 was introduced in 1955, and at the same time there were modifications to the electrics.

The Suburbanette was also introduced in 1955. This model was created especially for the United States, and was only ever sold there. It had a smaller front mudguard and smaller running boards than its sibling, and less side panelling. Instead of two foam seats, the Suburbanette was fitted with a single seat for two people.

These weight-saving devices gave the little Zündapp a top speed of just over 100kph (62mph). Alas, the Americans did not prefer the Suburbanette to the home-grown product, and only 370 were ever sold.

With sales of the Bella going well (18,000 of the original 150cc and 27,000 of the more powerful 200cc machines) Zündapp considered bringing out a 125cc to complement the range. In the event, however, they decided that it was more cost-effective to give the Bella some up-

The 150cc Bella series started life with the headlamp midway between handlebars and mudguard. (Bella R153 1956)

dates and modifications instead. The R151 and R201 arrived for 1955, with a reinforced legshield with more rounded styling, plus a new carburettor and an improved cooling arrangement. Fittings for a Steib sidecar were introduced as an option: the Bella's sturdiness and size made it an ideal candidate for a combination unit. Almost 30,000 of the 151/201 series were manufactured, over 90 per cent of them the 200cc version.

The following year brought the R153, with a slightly more powerful 8hp engine, and the R203. Both were now fitted with swing-fork suspension, attached to a single hydraulic shock absorber. 19,000 R203s were manufactured, but only 6000 R153s (this including a number of examples of a special export version for the USA which, while well received by the press, did not sell so very well). The R204 and R154 were introduced in 1957, the former now with greater power - 12hp - and a top speed of 110kph (65mph). 14,000 R204s and 12,000 R154s were manufactured, again

including a USA export version. The last 150cc Bellas were made in 1958, although the 200cc continued, with a new 13hp version (now known simply as the Bella 200) appearing in 1961. A new 11hp 175cc model was introduced alongside it, both continuing until 1964. During this period 3500 of the 200 and 1000 of the 175 were made. Production ended in 1964, a total of more than 130,000 Bellas having been produced in all.

One of the major selling points had been quality. 'Every part of the Zündapp is

The sturdy Bellas were made for two: the pillion passenger had room to travel in comfort. Inset: access to the engine made relatively simple. (Bella R201 1956)

With the arrival of the R201, the Bella's front styling changed to a slightly more rounded shape. (Bella R201 1956)

made with expert precision and craftsmanship,' boasted the advertising. 'Zündapp enjoys a worldwide reputation based on sound engineering principles. The proven reliability of Zündapp makes it the safest machine on the road. Brakes, lights, road-holding ability, cushion-ride and powerful performance give the rider utmost confidence in its handling even over the most rugged terrain.'

After the Bella, Zündapp followed the trend for small, slimmed-down scooters with the introduction of the 50 and the RS50, which were very similar in style to the slim-line Vespas and Lambrettas of the period. With their handlebar gearchange and smaller wheels, they moved away from a motorcycling past towards a younger market. However, the little 50cc Zündapps did not trigger a renaissance. The company stayed in business for another twenty years, selling in that time about the same number of units as the popular Bella had managed in half the time. The writing was on the wall for Zündapp; production ceased, and the factory contents were sold, lock, stock and barrel, to China. But the Bella is not forgotten. Sporting its friendly daisy motif where other scooters wear impersonal crests and shields, the Bella has a huge following today, in Germany, around Europe, and throughout the rest of the world.

Elegant two-tone colour schemes were available for the Bella: lighter panels (where darker ones might have been expected) changed the scooter's whole appearance and,

here, the effect is enhanced with whitewall tyres.
(Bella R203 1957)

The Bella daisy motif was an unusual choice, and easily recognised.
(Bella R203 1957)

The later Bellas were favoured with a reshaped handlebar section and indicators.
(Bella 200 1962)

The rear seat hinged neatly for access to the fuel filler.
(Bella 200: 1962)

Unlike some other makes, everything is easy to reach.
(Bella 200: 1962)

Four wheels bad; two wheels good? It was not always simply an economic decision. If scootering began as a purely practical proposition, it soon became much more for those who were hooked. (Bella 200 1962)

PHOTOGRAPHER'S POSTSCRIPT

For twenty years I have worked with Leica cameras and lenses, which I suppose counts as some sort of testimonial. In our book about Lambrettas I wrote about the advantages of zoom lenses, and my reluctance to use them. Well, all the pictures in this book were made with the two Leica zooms and a fish-eye. I need not have worried!

In the Lambretta Family Album I also mentioned my debt of thanks to Mike and Val Dan, and I must report that they are stars still, and have been of huge help in supplying machines and information. One of the highlights of working on this book was the trip to Brussels, accompanied by Val and Mike, to visit the home of the Belgian Piattis. Bart Eeman was charm itself, and nothing was too much trouble. I am indebted to him for access to the Paitti archive, as well as for allowing me to photograph the two machines from the museum. Still with Piatti, I must thank the models Tina Forkel and Sandra de Silva. Jane Palmer, Marketing Manager of Bristol Zoo, very kindly made the zoo available as a background, and I must say how impressed I was with its animal and human friendliness.

My thanks also to Martin van der Langenburg for his time and energy, and for an excellent tour of Arnhem! His knowledge of things IWL is immense, and he introduced me to Jan Vellinga, Harold van Hees, Gunter

The Zündapp Bella - Frost! (Bella R204 1960)

van Herreweghen and also Hans van Beek of the Zündapp Bella club in the Netherlands. Hans, I must say is an enthusiast of the highest order, and it was a pleasure to work with him and to meet his charming family. He put me in touch with Jan Jansen, who owns what is now a real rarity in the shape of a Bitri scooter.

My overriding memory of that shoot is of the intense cold that comes from working in the wilds of a flat country, in strong easterly wind, in mid-December. Nathalie van der Klok had kindly agreed to be a model, having featured in the Custom VW Family Album, with another Custom VW escapee, Bert Woolfink, kindly providing the much-needed translation service! We spent an hour drinking coffee afterwards - warmth and good company - a little piece of heaven! My thanks to Mario Piscicelli for allowing me to photograph his beautiful Bellas, and Jaak Kerkhofs and his lovely wife for their Troll.

The Gilera scooters were supplied by Piaggio UK, and I would like to thank Shirley Pattison, who has shown a continuing interest in our projects ever since she helped with our Vespa book. Pauline Chart, complete with red hair, froze almost solid during a particularly icy shoot. And so, finally, to France. It was at a meeting in Lomme, near Lille, that I renewed my acquaintance with Alain Goulois, of the French Lambretta Club, who had a stand at the show. My thanks also to the Lomme scooter dealers who very kindly let me photograph several modern Peugeots. Marie-Laurence Decke, Florence Boyer and Patrick Pattier added their considerable charms and humour.

While in France I met Marc Defrance, whose Jet 200 was featured in the Lambretta book. He introduced me to Yves Dumetz, and arranged a photoshoot for later in the year. Unfortunately, at the time of the shoot M. Dumetz was ill, and had to go to hospital, but Marc and his friend, Freddy, were there to manhandle his scooters. Another session later saw us working on some of Marc's collection with help from the lovely Catherine Skrzypczak. At the end of the day Marc insisted on cooking a meal for Andrea and myself ... and by the time we left, the stars were out. Thank you all.

David Sparrow